Dedicated to my amazing mum, whose kindness, humour and strength were matched only by her organisational skills. x

Acknowledgements

Writing an acknowledgements page feels very surreal but is a welcome opportunity to extend thanks to some of the people who have helped me along the way.

Firstly, thank you to Anne MacIntosh at Business Gateway for all her help on my business journey. She has been a sounding board, a shoulder to cry on and a huge champion of all things Better Organised.

Fate played a hand when I met Kim Macleod of Indie Authors World! She has supported me personally and professionally as this book has taken shape. Her guidance and expertise have kept me on track throughout the writing and publishing process and I am forever grateful.

It has been a privilege to work with many wonderful clients over the last few years and I am so grateful to them for trusting me with their homes, businesses and emotions.

Huge thanks to everyone at the Association of Professional Declutterers & Organisers (APDO). I was chuffed to bits to discover my tribe and am so proud to be part of something that truly changes lives! #colleaguesnotcompetitors

I'm in the fortunate position of being able to say that the friends, collaborators and supporters who've been alongside me on my business journey are too many to mention. Suffice to say, I feel so lucky to know you - your backing doesn't go unnoticed!

I sincerely appreciate all the encouragement from Dad and Joanne. Thank you for 'getting it' when I said that I was setting up Better Organised and I now understand some of what you have experienced as fellow business owners.

Neil, Emma and Matthew – your unwavering support keeps me sane, focused and motivated. From listening to my decluttering chat to accompanying me on charity shop drop-offs and helping spread the word about Better Organised, I can't ask for better team-mates and I love you all to bits .

INTRODUCTION

Hi! I'm Kate. I live just outside Glasgow, Scotland, with my husband, daughter and son, and for as long as I can remember I have loved all things organised. From stationery supplies to Sindy dolls, I grew up with a 'place for everything' approach. This stood me in good stead for my late teens, when my mum sadly passed away after a long illness. My dad, sister and I pulled together as a team to keep the household running as efficiently as Mum had, and I really came to appreciate how her organised approach had been such an integral part of our family home. I couldn't believe how much had to be done to keep things ticking over and I quickly realised that having simple, logical systems and routines in place made all the difference when it came to basic tasks such as meal planning, shopping, laundry and housework.

I have worked since I was 12, and looking back at my jobs I can see the common theme is that I'm happiest when I am using my organisational skills to support other people, whether that be as a PA, a human resources advisor or as a volunteer for an international charity.

When I became a mum, the benefits of an organised approach struck me again. From studiously preparing for the arrival of my daughter to ensuring changing bags were well stocked, bottles were sterilised and activities were planned, I became increasingly aware that the more organised I was, the more positive and capable I felt during that busy period of adjustment.

After a spell as a stay-at-home mum I was preparing to return to the workforce and was delighted to discover the professional organising industry, and in particular the Association of Professional Declutterers & Organisers (APDO)! I have always loved decluttering and organising and have previously done it for friends and family, as well as in my own home, so it was exciting to blend this passion with my administrative skills and commit to starting my own business as a professional organiser & PA.

I now support clients in their home or business, by assisting them with their organisational challenges, such as hands-on decluttering, help with paperwork, diary management or support with a house move.

Every day I am fortunate to work on exciting projects with lovely clients. Their homes, lifestyles and circumstances can differ significantly, but they all have busy lives and want to enjoy a more comfortable level of organisation. I feel privileged to be invited into their home or business to help them bridge the gap from overwhelmed to organised.

I could write a whole book about the benefits of an organised approach but I think the main ones are;

› A sense of clarity – you know what you have and where it is

› Space and safety – taking control of your surroundings has the possibility to free up physical space, which not only makes your home tidier but also means a safer home with less obstructions

› It saves time – knowing where to find things and being able to access them quickly and easily means no more minutes are wasted in searching for things. A tidy and organised home also take less time to clean!

› You save money – from decluttering your direct debits, memberships and subscriptions to being more mindful about what you buy and no longer buying duplicates of items you already have, you'd be surprised how much you can potentially save by taking a more organised path

› A tidy house = a tidy mind – an orderly and calming environment makes it easier to relax and enjoy your home

Do you long for a lifestyle without physical and mental clutter but don't know where to begin? Are you looking for a comfortable, sustainable level of organisation but want some guidance on how to go about it? Then you've come to the right place!

I have written this book to help you to streamline and simplify your home. This is not a prescriptive technique but a friendly, flexible approach that can be adapted to suit you and your surroundings. It covers thirty categories – from shoes to stationery to smartphones and everything in between – and I've broken everything down into manageable bite-sized chunks. Please think of the categories and steps as prompts rather than strict instructions. There is no need to tackle every category in thirty consecutive days (unless you want to, of course!) or to approach them in a set order. You can simply dip in and out of the plan as time, energy and focus dictate.

I'm so passionate about supporting you to achieve the clarity, calm and productivity that comes from a streamlined environment. One of my favourite phrases is 'reduce until something clicks', as it perfectly sums up the Better Organised approach. I don't dictate one in, one out or letting go of a specific number of items, but rather finding your own sense of 'lagom' (not too much, not too little, just right). The actual amount of possessions and commitments you have is so individual. You will have your own sense of how much, or little, feels comfortable for you, but I sincerely hope that what follows will give you the tools and motivation to make the most of your precious space and time, so that you have the freedom to focus on the things that are most important to you!

P.S. If you want to get a head-start, set up a donation station for items to be donated to charity. It can be a cardboard box under the stairs, a basket in the hall or a toy chest on the landing - just something reasonably sized and empty!

"Have nothing in your house that you do not know to be useful or believe to be beautiful."

William Morris

DAY 01

Photograph by Julius Drost

Purses and Wallets

Are you ready to get going with the 30 day plan? Today we kick off with a quick and easy place to start — your purse/wallet!

- Empty the contents out onto a table or worktop
- Check receipts and discard any that are no longer required. File the rest
- Look at expiry dates on coupons and vouchers, disposing of any that are no longer valid. Check dates on gift cards and make a note to use them before they run out
- Consider whether you need to keep all the loyalty cards that you carry in your purse. Cancel any that you simply never use, or consider using an app such as Stocard to keep digital copies
- Could any of your credit or store cards be kept elsewhere? Leaving them at home when you go shopping might mean you're less tempted to buy on impulse!
- Once you've removed the clutter from your purse just pop the remaining items back in and that's day 1's challenge done!

Top tip *- I only keep a receipt in my purse until I see the transaction appear on my online banking. That lets me keep tabs on how much is due to come out of my account but minimises the bits of paper in my purse. I only retain receipts long-term for business purposes or if the item is expensive i.e. electrical items.*

DAY 02

Photograph by StockSnap

Junk Drawers

Day 2 is time to tackle the dreaded junk drawer! Do you have a drawer that is overflowing with random keys, old cables, unused stationery items and out of date medication? Here are a few simple steps to getting it under control!

- Empty the drawer onto a worktop and immediately set aside anything that definitely needs kept (spare car keys!)
- Safely discard any out of date medicines or vitamins
- Dispose of anything that is obviously redundant — dried out elastic bands, pens that no longer work etc.
- Use items that you have around the house to group and organise what is left — shoe box lids, empty jewellery boxes, business card boxes, clean/shallow candle jars and Ferrero Rocher boxes are all great for containing similar items together. Alternatively, adjustable drawer dividers are easy to pick up from Amazon or Ikea
- Assign items to their appropriate containers and pop it all back in the drawer

Voila! A neat and organised drawer - no more junk.

Top tip *– Electrical cables, redundant chargers and old batteries can be taken to your local recycling centre. Alternatively, many of the large electrical retailers, such as Currys, have drop-off points in store for items to be recycled.*

DAY 03

Photograph by Milada Vigerova

Windowsills

Day 3 is a chance to clear the clutter from all of your windowsills - let the fresh air in and literally get things flowing!

This was a suggestion I picked up from another professional organiser - when she arrives to start work at a new client's home she suggests starting with a brief declutter of windowsills, as they're usually straightforward to do, results are seen quickly and opening the windows immediately creates a positive shift in energy!

› Gather everything from the windowsill, dispose of any litter such as sweet wrappers or opened envelopes and throw open the window

› Go through the remaining items and decide if any can be donated or discarded - do you still love your ornaments and knick knacks? Anything that's not staying but is in good condition can go in your donation station for delivery to the charity shop

› If there are items that don't belong on the windowsill return them to their home (CDs, nail polish, letters, toys etc.)

› Give the area a quick clean and enjoy the clear, clutter-free view

Top tip *– Consider using vertical space for convenient storage. Wall-mounted units, shelves, over-door racks and hooks can all keep items within easy reach whilst minimising windowsill clutter.*

DAY 04

Photograph by 3dman_eu

Medicines and First Aid

Day 4 brings an opportunity to purge your medicines and first aid box.

› Gather all of your medicines and first aid supplies - remember to include children's medicines and anything that you keep in toiletry bags, baby changing bags or the car

› Set aside anything that has passed its expiry date; both prescription and over the counter medications can become ineffective or even toxic once they are out of date

› Also set aside any medicines that look discoloured, separated or dried out

› Pop the remaining items back into a clear plastic box (pound shops, supermarkets and Ikea usually stock good ranges), shoebox or basket

› Medicines that are no longer needed, out of date or damaged should be taken to your local pharmacy for safe disposal

› Do a stock check of your first aid box and if anything is running low add it to a shopping list

Top tip *– Ensure products are stored according to manufacturer's instructions and group like with like i.e. plasters and dressings, gels and liquid medicines, children's items, so that it's easy to see at a glance what you have and avoid stockpiles building up.*

DAY 05

Photograph from Adobe Stock

Toiletries

Day 5 - a chance to take a fresh look at your toiletries.

- Empty bathroom cupboards and pull out toiletries from bedroom drawers, around the bath or any other areas of the house
- Dispose of anything that has expired or is leaking
- Set aside any items that are unopened and unwanted - homeless shelters will be grateful for these
- Most charity shops accept unopened gift sets
- If you have partially used bottles of the same product then combine them to save space
- If you have amassed a collection of samples or travel size products consider leaving them in view so that you make a point of using them before buying any more full size products
- Clean the area where toiletries are stored and then place those that you are currently using within easy reach

Top tip - *Clear plastic boxes are ideal for grouping and storing toiletries. Standing items upright lets you see what you have at a glance and makes it easier to avoid stockpiling duplicates.*

DAY 06

Photograph by element5

Make up

Day 6 - we're looking at decluttering make up.

- Empty ALL of your make up onto a worktop or the kitchen table, remembering to include any from drawers, handbags and make up bags
- Group types of products together - foundations, powders, lipsticks - to give you a clear view of how much you have of each thing
- Ditch anything that is out of date, dried up or that you know you will never use
- Bear in mind that, as a general rule, most liquid make up shouldn't be kept longer than six months once opened, as it can harbour germs
- Be really honest about what you actually use. You could give new products to a friend or sell them on eBay. Alternatively, women's and homeless shelters will gladly accept unopened items that are in good condition. The charity Give & Make Up will accept some lightly used second-hand make-up, with the exception of lip glosses and mascara
- Try to use up existing products before purchasing any similar ones
- Wash your make up brushes (baby shampoo is ideal for this) and pop your make up bag in the washing machine, if it is a washable fabric

Top tip *- Keep a small make up bag at the location where you normally put your make up on, keeping only the items you use daily. Keep party make up in a separate location so that you're not rummaging through it every day to find your regular mascara!*

DAY
07

Cleaning products

Day 7 of our challenge already! Time to come clean...

- Gather all of your cleaning products together - the ones from under the sink, the utility room, your cleaning caddy and anywhere else in the house - and do a quick stock check
- Combine products where you have half-full bottles of the same product
- Put aside anything that you know you will never use - leather cleaner, upholstery cleaner, Brasso and wood cleaner are all items that might have been lurking under the sink but never seen the light of day! Perhaps a friend or family member could use them? Alternatively, you could sell them at a car boot sale or donate them to your local church or charity
- If you use laundry tabs or dishwasher tabs, storing them in clear containers makes it easy to see when you are running low - just remember to label the container and keep it out of reach of children
- Give the area a quick clean, group similar products together and place them back in their home. Plastic boxes/baskets or large ice cream tubs are ideal

Top tip - *Try using a Lazy Susan turntable for easy access to your everyday products! Amazon stocks a nice range from InterDesign.*

DAY 08

Photograph by kaboompics

Diaries & Schedules

Day 8 is one of my personal favourites as we look to the week ahead - diaries & schedules!

For simplifying your schedule and giving you some headspace, a review of diary commitments can be a worthwhile exercise. Busyness can be contagious but are you overbooked, overtired and overwhelmed? Then cull with confidence!

- Flick through your diary/calendar to identify what your real priorities and genuine commitments are. Determining which activities are non-negotiable is a great starting point. These might be some kids' activities, a regular get together with friends, or an evening class that you take
- Are there any commitments that you can say no to? Or that can be delegated, shared or outsourced? If so, now is a good opportunity to 'spring clean' your schedule so that you have time to focus more on the things that you really want to be doing
- Setting aside 10 minutes on a Sunday evening to do a weekly review can be a really effective way to keep on top of commitments and activities, getting you clear and current on what's coming up and providing an opportunity to prepare for the week ahead, gather your thoughts in advance of meetings or events, to remind yourself of appointments and to take a note of upcoming birthdays (and presents/cards to buy!)

Top tip *- As well as one-off activities, I put all regular commitments (with the exception of school and work!) in my diary i.e. clubs, after school activities, exercise classes. I add a note to indicate if it is the last one of the term, as this makes it easy to plan for the weeks that an activity isn't on and also acts as a heads-up that payment will be due for the next block!*

DAY 09

Photograph by Jason Leung

Store cupboard

Day 9 - we are in the kitchen for the next few days!

- Gather dry ingredients, packets, jars, cans and bottles from your kitchen cupboards and lay them out on the table
- Remember to include herbs and spices and any food/drink items that are kept in utility rooms, garages or sheds
- Check expiry dates and dispose of anything that is past its use by date
- When reviewing what's left, be really honest about what you will actually use and consider donating unopened items to your local food bank - most supermarkets have collection points in-store
- Group similar types of items together and, where possible, pop into appropriate containers - baskets, shoe boxes and tupperwares are all handy for neatly corralling foodstuffs and make it easy to see what you have (and therefore minimise unnecessary purchasing)
- Clean and dry the inside of the cupboard before placing items back in

Top tip *- Use high shelves for storing seldom used products and duplicate items, keeping frequently used (and therefore frequently replenished) items at eye level.*

DAY 10

Photograph by Jenny Pace

Utensils

Day 10 and we are getting to grips with kitchen paraphernalia!

- Empty all utensils and cutlery onto the kitchen table and immediately set aside anything that is definitely being kept. Think carefully about how many of the same item you need, particularly when it comes to cutlery!
- Sort through the remaining items, discarding anything that is broken and putting together a pile of items that can be donated to charity
- Perhaps think about letting go of items where you have two things that do the same job i.e. peelers, knives, graters
- Take a moment to do a little stock-check of tupperwares and tubs - will you ever use it if you don't have a lid for it?
- A quick check of your gadgets is worth doing too - if you never use something then perhaps it is time to give it a new lease of life with a different owner? Ebay and Gumtree are obvious choices if you wish to sell, or donate items to your local charity shop (just check which ones accept electrical items)

Top tip *- I recommend keeping all utensils and cutlery in drawers – this avoids food splatters and dust accumulating on them and leaves counter-tops relatively clear and easy to clean.*

DAY 11

Photograph by Brooke Lark

Plates and Bowls

Day 11 is a chance to edit your crockery.

- Take plates and bowls out of your cupboards, including serving dishes
- Remove anything that is cracked, chipped or not fit for purpose. Think carefully about whether to keep things that are not used, ugly or difficult to clean
- Set to one side anything that can be donated to charity
- Consider how many you need of each item and edit accordingly
- Do you keep certain items for special occasions only? Perhaps keep them easily accessible and enjoy using them on a regular basis!
- Give the shelves a quick clean and dry before placing your edited collection back on them

Top tip - *If you have inherited/been gifted items that simply don't suit your taste or lifestyle and have therefore never been used, take this opportunity to make a final decision on whether they should stay. Be practical and honest and consider letting them go to auctions or charity to free up precious storage space in your home. If the items have sentimental value, take some photos of them before you let them go.*

DAY 12

Fridge and Freezer

Day 12 and we delve into the fridge & freezer.

- Remove everything and lay it out on the kitchen table or worktop, discarding anything that is out of date or that you know you will never use
- Wipe down shelves and drawers
- Consider moving fridge shelves up or down, if possible, to use the space most efficiently
- Group items i.e. sauces, cheeses, kids' snacks etc., putting them in plastic baskets if you have any to hand
- Assigning categories to each drawer in the freezer can work really well, as you see at a glance what is running low - I split it into veg, proteins, carbs and desserts/fruit
- Putting fruit & veg at eye level in the fridge can encourage you to use them while they are fresh, while putting children's items in the salad drawers means the kids can easily help themselves to a snack
- Glass jars are ideal for leftovers, chopped veg or salad portions

Top tip *- If you're looking to minimise visual clutter, remove magnets, letters and pictures that are stored on the fridge door.*

DAY 13

Photograph by David Becker

Glasses and Mugs

Day 13 is a chance to take a fresh look at your glasses, cups and mugs.

- Gather all of the above onto the worktop, discarding any that are chipped or cracked
- Wipe down shelves
- Group like with like - tumblers, wine glasses etc., and assess how many you have. Also consider how many you need when entertaining
- When it comes to mugs, think about how many people in your home use them and how many are typically used in a day. Could any surplus ones be repurposed as holders for stationery items, pens, tools or make up brushes?
- Set aside those that will be sent to charity
- Before putting items back in the cupboard, have a look at the height of the shelf and decide whether moving it up or down would give you some more functional room and get rid of dead space
- Pop the kettle on and enjoy a cuppa while admiring another clutter free zone!

Top tip *- Place glasses of varying heights in rows from front to back instead of storing tall glasses behind smaller ones across the width of the cabinet. This makes it easy to reach for a glass of any size.*

DAY 14

Photograph by Mel Poole

Bedding and Towels

Day 14 brings a chance to purge the linen cupboard.

- Empty everything out of the cupboard and onto the floor or bed
- Consider how often you rotate your towels and how frequently you do laundry - as a guide, 2 sets of towels per person plus 2 guest sets will usually be enough for most households (plus 2 - 3 hand towels per bathroom/WC)
- Set aside any that are being discarded/donated
- Group the remaining items 'like with like', fold neatly and pop them back in the cupboard
- If space is tight in the linen cupboard, consider storing beach towels in vacuum bags or lidded plastic boxes in the attic/under the bed...or simply keep them in your suitcases if you know you'll only ever use them when you go away on holiday
- Follow the same process for bedding

Top tip **-** *Some animal shelters and homeless charities accept used towels and bedding that is in reasonable condition - call ahead to check that your local branch will take them.*

DAY 15

Photograph by Rodion Kutsaev

Smartphones

Day 15 of the plan and you don't even need to leave the sofa - it's time to declutter your phone!

- Delete unused apps, old messages and out of date contacts - anything that is distracting or using up precious memory
- Go through the photos and purge any outtakes or shots that you know you don't want to keep. Consider moving the remaining photos off your phone and into cloud storage or an external device
- Turn off useless push notifications for things that you don't need to be reminded about
- Consider deleting any books, music or other downloads that you no longer need
- Depending on your phone model, you'll probably be able to set up app folders to keep items grouped together and off your main screen
- The Moment app can automatically track how much you use your phone and lets you set up screen time for all the family

Top tip - *Only keep messages that require an action or response and delete the rest. This can be a really effective way of staying clear and focussed on what is current and means you're not wasting time scrolling through previous conversations.*

DAY 16

Photograph by Kelly Sikkema

Hats, Scarves and Gloves

Day 16 of the plan and we turn towards clothing, starting with hats, scarves & gloves.

- Lay out all hats, scarves and gloves; remember to include those from the car/garage/schoolbags

- Group each family member's items together

- Immediately put aside any that can be donated to charity (clothing banks are ideal for these items, as some charity shops won't accept off-season clothing due to lack of space)

- Do a quick inventory of what is left. Tuck gloves and a scarf inside each hat so that it is easy to grab a set before leaving the house in the morning - 2 sets per family member is usually enough

Consider whether now is the time to pack away seasonal gear and pull out the next season's hats and accessories!?

Top tip - *A basket or over-the-door shoe organiser in the hall cupboard is convenient for keeping accessories neat and easily accessible for kids and adults alike.*

Photograph by Jakob Owens

Shoes and Boots

Day 17 brings us on to shoes & boots. This might be part of a bigger project, particularly when you include off-season or occasion wear (I've previously worked with a client to streamline a collection of over 300 pairs of shoes), so if time is tight simply focus on your regular everyday footwear for now.

› Gather your shoes together and group roughly by type - work shoes, trainers, pumps etc. You might be surprised by how many you have that are very similar!

› Give the area a quick clean while it is empty

› Select those shoes that are definite keepers and put them to one side

› Grab any that are at the end of their shelf life and discard

› Go through the ones that are left and consider whether or not they should be kept. If in doubt, check whether they fit, are comfortable and if you still have outfits that go well with them

› Pop items to be donated into a bag for the charity shop/clothing bank

› Before putting items back in your wardrobe think about how they are stored and consider whether you are making the best use of the space - if there is a lot of dead space then adjusting a shelf or using clear, stackable plastic boxes can work well

Top tip - *Off season shoes don't need to take up room in your daily space - perhaps have a seasonal box stored elsewhere. If you unpack/swap the off-season stuff twice a year it's a good chance to naturally declutter (I usually do it around the times the clocks change).*

DAY
18

Underwear, Socks and Tights

Day 18 and a chance to sort through underwear & socks!

- Tip items out on to the bed and group by type - pants, bras, socks, tights
- Consider setting aside occasion wear (strapless bras, shape wear) and storing it elsewhere - perhaps in a clear plastic box on a high shelf of your wardrobe
- Discard anything that you no longer like or that doesn't fit - if items are clean but no longer in wearable condition they can be donated to clothing banks for textile recycling
- If you have unworn items that still have labels/are in their original packaging they can be donated to charity shops
- Drawer dividers can be handy for keeping items neatly organised (shoe boxes without lids work well for this, as does packaging from toiletry gift sets)
- Pair and ball socks, roll tights and fold bras in half to be stored vertically
- Place items back into the drawer in general categories

Top tip - *Keep it simple! For your everyday items, consider having only one colour of socks and pants and having the same style of bra in two colours i.e. 2 black and 2 white. This takes up less room and means you can easily see at a glance if you are running low. When assessing how many you need, do bear in mind your laundry schedule – the more often you do washing, the fewer items you will need!*

DAY 19

Photograph by Will Malott

Clothing

Day 19 of the plan is a fresh look at clothing.

This is likely to be part of a significant project, so for now perhaps just choose one category to start with and work through the steps below. Maybe your wardrobe is overflowing with tops, you have a collection of dresses that gather dust or your hall cupboard is bursting at the seams with unworn coats and jackets. If you don't know where to start, go with the area that you access most frequently and you'll hopefully find the others will follow.

› Lay all of the items on your bed or floor, grouping roughly by type (i.e. workwear, casual etc).

› Select the items which you know you definitely want to keep - those that you love wearing and that fit comfortably

› Go through the remaining items and set aside any that can be donated to charity or discarded

› If anything is in need of repair lay it to one side but be really honest with yourself about whether you have the time and energy to repair it yourself or take it to an alterations shop!

› Give the inside of the wardrobe or drawer a quick clean and dry before putting items back inside

› Consider grouping by type and/or colour - skinny hangers are a brilliant space-saver to keep things neatly ordered and make it easy to see what you have

***Top tip** - Check pockets and compartments for cash or belongings before bagging up items for donation!*

DAY 20

Photograph by baby-natur

Kids' Clothing

Day 20 of the 30-day plan and a chance to streamline kids' clothing!

If time is tight, just choose one category (i.e. tops, dresses, trousers). Perhaps leave seasonal/occasional wear for now and only focus on the everyday items.

- Lay all of the items on a bed or floor
- Select the pieces that are in reasonable condition and that still fit comfortably
- Go through the remaining items and set aside any that can be donated to a friend or charity, or that need discarded
- If anything is in need of repair lay it to one side, but be really honest with yourself about whether you have the time and energy to repair it yourself or take it to an alterations shop!
- Give the inside of the wardrobe or drawer a quick clean and dry before putting items back inside
- Consider grouping by type and/or colour - extendable, adjustable hangers are an inexpensive way to keep kids' clothing neatly ordered

Top tip - *Consider having a too big/too small box for storing items that will be worn at a later date or that will be handed down to younger children. If you roughly group the items by type/size then a regular review of the contents can mean less unnecessary purchasing when existing items are outgrown. It's also handy as a place to store things that you pick up in end of season sales!*

DAY 21

Photograph by Alfonso Ramirez

Bags & Accessories

Day 21 is an opportunity to take a fresh look at bags & accessories. Depending on time and energy levels, you might want to choose one category to start with - everyday bags, clutch bags or belts perhaps - but if time allows consider looking at overnight bags, beach bags, kids' bags and backpacks too.

- Lay items out and roughly group by category and colour (you might be surprised to see how many black evening bags you have!)
- Check the condition and have a look in pockets and compartments
- Consider whether each bag is still fit for purpose, if it's a style you like and when you last used it
- Some options for storing bags are; handbag racks, over the door holders or hooks. Magazine holders or shelf dividers work well for clutch bags
- Packing bags with tissue paper will keep them upright and help them retain their shape
- Set aside anything for charity or to sell - designer bags hold their value well!

Top tip - *Apparently women spend an average of 10 minutes a day rummaging in their handbags to find things. A handbag organiser can be a good way of keep items organised and is easily transferred between bags, or simply minimise the number of things you keep in your bag.*

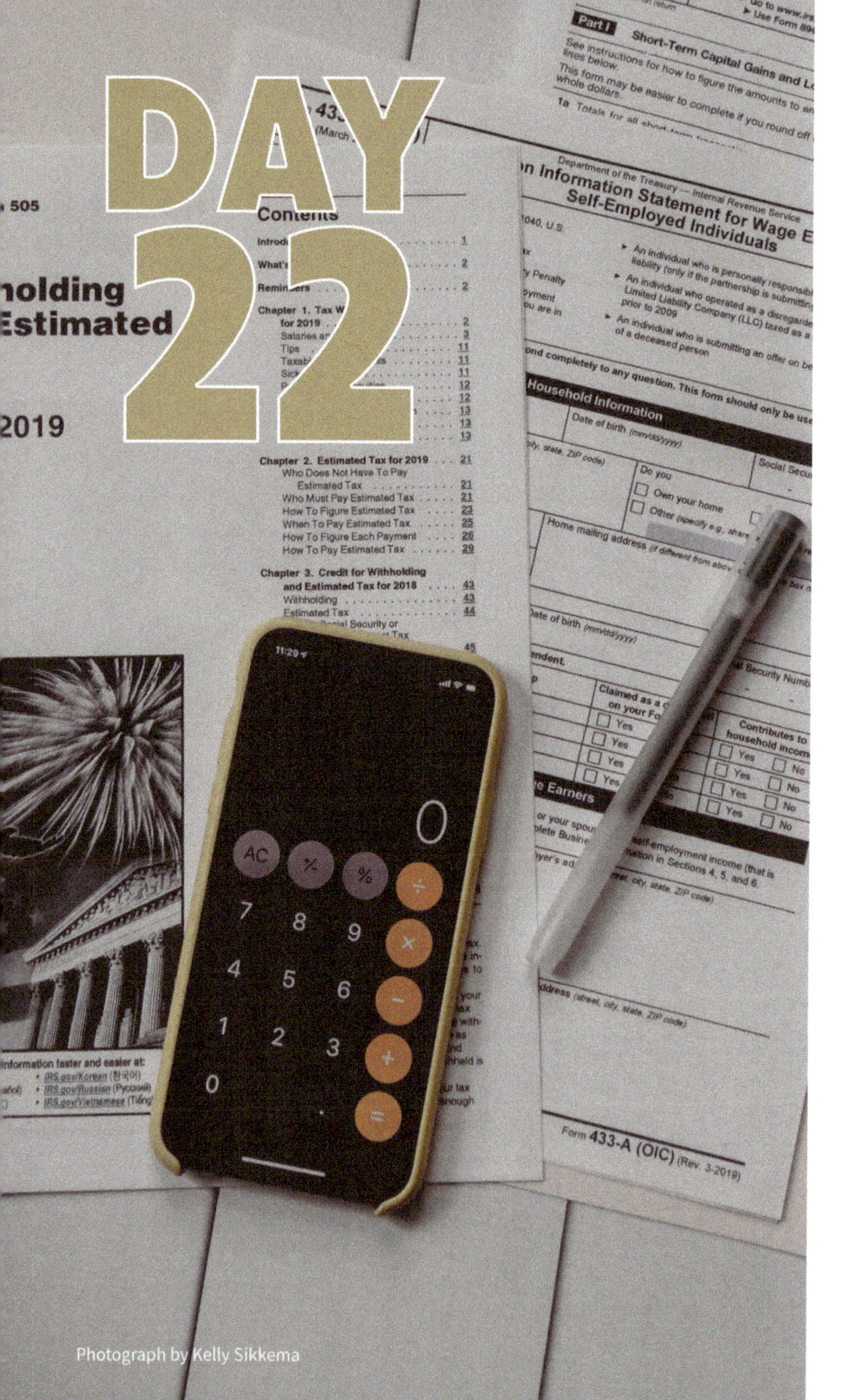

DAY 22

Photograph by Kelly Sikkema

Paperwork

Day 22 of the plan is an opportunity to streamline and simplify household paperwork. Having a basic system in place can help you stay up-to-date and able to lay your hands on documents quickly.

- Designate an area for items that are in progress i.e. party invitations, letters about upcoming activities or trips, bills to be paid, gift vouchers/season tickets, and anything else that requires an action or response
- An expanding file works well for the above - ideally located somewhere easily accessible i.e. a kitchen worktop or a drawer in the living room
- A quick review once a week will usually be enough to keep you clear and current and provides a chance to recycle/shred where appropriate
- Identify a suitable location for all other paperwork i.e. a filing cabinet, box or drawers. Items filed here might include insurance policies, utility bills, wills, passports, birth certificates and car-related documents. General categories and simple labels are usually enough to keep things in order
- Depending on how much time is available, either gather together all your paperwork or take a file/category at a time and start sorting into piles; recycle, shred or file
- If you don't have a shredder, an ID protection roller stamp is an alternative - it will hide your personal information and the document can then be placed in recycling
- Anything that is being kept can be filed away or put in the 'in progress' area

Top tip *- An A4 storage box is ideal for storing guarantees and warranties. If I buy a new item I attach the receipt to the front of the instruction manual and drop it into the box. I have a quick look through it once or twice a year and recycle anything that is no longer required.*

DAY 23

Photograph by Frans Van Heerden

Stationery

Day 23 is a chance to purge stationery items. If you're tight for time, perhaps do kids' stationery separately!

› Gather stationery items from around the home and group by category

› Discard anything that doesn't work i.e. dried out Tippex

› Consider whether you'll use remaining items, particularly where you have duplicates, such as bull dog clips or hole punches

› Unwanted items can be donated to nurseries, start up businesses or local arts groups, or bundled for sale online or at car boot sales

› Alternatively, look at Pens for Kids or School Aid if you want to donate items to schools and orphanages here or overseas. Items for School Aid can be dropped off at The Entertainer stores nationwide by prior arrangement

› Pop remaining items back where they belong. Apple product boxes and their lids make great drawer dividers for containing stationery bits & bobs

Top tip *- Unused planners, notebooks and folders are loved by kids or will be gratefully received by guide groups, community groups or nurseries.*

DAY 24

Photograph by Pixabay

Gift Wrap and Cards

Day 24 of the plan is a quick and easy category - gift wrap and cards!

- Gather together all your wrapping materials, including paper, bows and ribbon. Include greetings cards and gift tags
- Set aside anything that is tatty or that you know you'll never use. Perhaps set up a little craft box for kids?
- Consider donating items in good condition to nurseries or local craft groups
- Items that are in unopened packaging can be donated to charity shops
- A deep rectangular basket is ideal for storing wrapping materials, with rolls of wrap stood upright. Shoe boxes or clear plastic boxes work well for cards, gift tags, bows etc. Keep it easily accessible, along with scissors, sellotape and stamps
- Having a little stock of generic or blank cards can be handy if you need one at short notice!

Top tip - *Do you struggle to remember birthdays and never seem to have a card to hand when you need one? Then consider buying and writing cards in batches. Once every three months, I'll sit and write cards for upcoming birthdays and events. I don't address them (in case the recipient moves before the event) but do put the name on the envelope. In the top right-hand corner, I write the date of the event. I then store them in date order and quickly flick through them once a week to stamp/post as and when required.*

DAY 25

Photograph by Sharon McCutcheon

Books

Day 25 brings us onto books. If your time is limited simply concentrate on one category for now - perhaps fiction, cookbooks or kids' books.

- Take books off shelves and have a good look to check for duplicates (bearing in mind any printed books that might be duplicated on a Kindle)
- Identify those that are non-negotiable - perhaps the ones that you love to read over and over, have inherited, are signed copies or first editions
- Decide how you would like them to be sorted/stored - alphabetically, by genre or perhaps rainbowtised! Or will you follow the latest trend for backwards books?
- Set aside any that you're passing on to friends, charity, nurseries, schools or care homes
- Are you in doubt about whether to keep something? If so, ask yourself 'if I lost it would I replace it?'
- If you'd prefer to sell unwanted books do just bear in mind that they often have a very minimal resale value, unless it is a rare or signed copy. Ebay, Amazon and We Buy Books are all avenues for selling online
- Consider having a 'yet to read' shelf and limiting the number of books/length of time they stay on it

Top tip - *If you have textbooks look for overlaps when it comes to topics and have a quick glance to see if the information is still relevant to you now!*

DAY 26

Photograph by Oxana Lyashenko

Toys and Games

Day 26 is a chance to start tackling toys & games! This can be an overwhelming thought, so break it down into categories and prioritise one for now, such as Lego, dolls or puzzles.

- Grab a shoebox or tupperware to use as a ‘mystery bits’ box
- Gather the toys together and lay them all out so you get a clear idea of how much you have
- Go through the items, discarding any that are broken and setting aside any that will be passed on to charity or friends. If you come across any random/unidentified pieces pop them in the mystery bits box until you have gone through everything
- Determine whether items are used, in good condition and age appropriate. Involve the kids in the decision-making as much as possible
- Consider setting aside a selection of items to be kept at a grandparents' home and/or for a 'once in a while box' which only gets brought out during holidays, sick days or snow days
- Ebay, Gumtree, FB groups and car boot sales are all good options for selling unwanted toys
- A few ideas for basic toy storage are flexitubs, baskets, Ikea Trofast drawers or Kallax cubes, under bed boxes on castors, ice cream tubs and biscuit tins

Top tip *- My test of good storage is whether I can throw (unbreakable) toys in it from across the room :-)*

DAY 27

Photograph by Phil Hearing

CDs and DVDs

Day 27 and we approach a section that is tricky for many, as we're moving onto CDs & DVDs! If you have a particularly large collection just deal with it in bite sized chunks, perhaps a couple of shelves at a time.

› Take items off shelves and lay them out, including any from the car or attic

› Check for any duplicates, bearing in mind that some physical copies might be duplicated in your downloads or streaming service

› Do you still have a CD player and/or DVD player? If not, will you ever listen to/watch the disc again?

› Ask yourself if you still use them, and if so do you enjoy them. Music Magpie is an easy option if you're letting go of items but want to get some money back for them. Listing can be quicker than going through eBay but the value you get for them is often significantly lower

Top tip *- Set storage limits for CDs and DVDs. Whether it is a couple of shelves, a rack or a storage tower, choose a space that you feel holds an amount you're comfortable with and then group discs in this area. Setting up one or two zones and sticking to them means it's easy to keep tabs on what you have and can encourage more mindful purchasing behaviour.*

DAY 28

Photograph by Kenny Luo

Car

Day 28 is one of my favourites, as we declutter the car!

- Clear out all rubbish, including old air fresheners
- Go through what's left and put things in a logical order - an old towel stored under the driver's seat and a packet of baby wipes in each of the pockets of the back doors always come in handy if you have kids (and can be used to give the dashboard and steering wheel a quick wipe)
- Muddy boots, dog leads and a first aid kit can probably live in the boot
- Consider keeping car documents and manuals in the glove compartment, along with hand sanitiser, hankies and sunglasses
- It can be worth keeping a couple of books and a few colouring supplies in the pockets on the back of the front seats
- Remove any items that don't need to be in the car; anything stored unnecessarily in the car adds to the weight and fuel consumption
- If time allows, a quick vacuum and a new air freshener are a nice finishing touch for a clutter-free car!

Top tip - *Keep some loose change in the car. This can come in handy for shopping trolley deposits and toll charges.*

DAY 29

Photograph by Rawpixel.com

Emails

Day 29 and there's no need to leave the comfort of your sofa. Whether you're a digital hoarder, strive for inbox zero or your emails are simply in need of a little spring clean, consider setting aside a little time to detox your inbox for enhanced clarity and focus!

- I generally avoid any permanent rules, flags or filters and keep it simple! Just set up a few folders, keeping categories fairly broad - holidays, car, kids etc.
- For sorting purposes here, filter emails by sender, deleting groups of messages if possible and moving the rest into the appropriate folders
- If a message requires an action, consider putting a reminder in your calendar or task list and filing the email (in Office, dragging an email straight into tasks creates a new task but the email is also kept and can be filed away)
- Do you get too many newsletters and daily deals? Take a little time to click the unsubscribe button at the bottom of those you no longer need, or adjust your preferences to get weekly highlights rather than a daily message
- If you are a Gmail user, Boomerang lets you schedule the sending of emails and can also remind you about a message with just one click - ideal if you want your memory to be refreshed about itinerary details just prior to travel
- Sanebox provides email management for any inbox and can be a particularly useful tool for business owners who are receiving a high volume of messages on a daily basis

Top tip - *Consider mirroring your folder set up for sent items too, only leaving messages in the original sent items area if they require an action or response. If updated regularly this is a simple but VERY effective reminder system and is the only one I use for keeping track of emails that might need chased up!*

DAY 30

Photograph by Ricardo Tamayo

Tech

Day 30 already! If there is one thing that often constitutes clutter it is redundant tech, so old mobiles, tablets and random cables and chargers can all be tackled today.

- Quickly go through drawers and storage to find anything that is no longer required. You might hit the jackpot so it's worth a quick look on eBay to see if your items are of significant value!
- Ensure that personal data is removed from phones and tablets
- If there are photos you want to keep transfer them to your current laptop or the cloud
- One of the most popular ways to pass on old mobiles and tablets is via the shops that sell them but other options include charities, Freecycle, auction sites or a service such as Mazuma Mobile. Alternatively, they can be taken to the small electrical section of your local recycling centre
- Discs are sometimes collected at local recycling centres but VHS tapes and cassettes are rarely accepted and are generally sent to landfill

Top tip - *It isn't usually necessary to keep original packaging for gadgets, mobile devices and appliances beyond the warranty period. Can you free up precious space in your attic or garage by purging some old packaging?!*

About the Author

Kate Galbally is a professional organiser & PA who's run her own business, Better Organised, since 2017. Following a long career in administrative support roles and a spell as a stay-at-home mum, she now makes a positive impact in other people's lives by giving them practical and emotional support to declutter and organise their home, business or schedule.

She is passionate about helping people go from overwhelmed to organised by assisting them to put simple, logical systems in place so that they can focus their time and energy on the things that are most important to them.

She has collaborated with brands such as Zero Waste Scotland, Hammonds, Avery UK, Small Business Saturday and Good Homes magazine.

Kate is a strong believer in keeping things simple and aiming for progress rather than perfection for a home that is calm, cosy and comfortable!

Contact info

Please contact Kate to sign up to her newsletter or enquire about speaking availability;

Website – www.betterorganised.uk

LinkedIn - www.linkedin.com/in/kategalbally/

For more tips, advice and motivation from Kate, please like her Facebook page: www.facebook.com/betterorganised/

www.ingramcontent.com/pod-product-compliance
Ingram Content Group UK Ltd.
Pitfield, Milton Keynes, MK11 3LW, UK
UKHW062307290726
14090UKWH00018B/936

9 781916 182905